Biking Through the Stone Age

Biking Through the Stone Age

Poems by

VA Smith

Cover design by Shay Culligan

ISBN: 978-1-63980-114-5

Kelsay Books
502 South 1040 East, A-119
American Fork, Utah 84003
Kelsaybooks.com

For Adrian, Sylvia, and Rosalyn—
story-tellers and change-makers

Thanks to William Keeney and Mary Rohrer-Dann
for their loving and astute reading of this manuscript
and to Sue Mathias and Lynda Goldstein for their
encouragement and support.

Acknowledgments

I thank the editors of the following publications in which these poems, some in different forms, first appeared:

Corvus Review: "Dancing with My Dead"

Evening Street Press and Review: "Welsh Mythology"

Parkinson's Poetry: "Garvey Manor"

Pure Slush: "Saturday Night"

Quartet: "Biking Through the Stone Age"

Silkworm: "Ocean City, New Jersey"

Uppagus: "Waking in Cluis"

Verdad: "Cuttings"

West Trade Review: "Ode to a Singular Phalaenopsis"

Yes, Poetry: "House Aria"

Ginosko Literary Review: "Birds of Philadelphia"

Contents

Biking through the Stone Age

Swiping sunscreen on
their soft necks and faces,
a strap check of their bike
hard-hats, my grandgirls
ask, again, about the before
times: *Were there helmets,*
Bin Bin, when you were a kid?

A proper grandmother might
offer nostalgia or longing:
No, those were simpler times,
kids not pampered or protected.
But none of us prize proper, all
three filled with sass and badass,
biking along the canal, frog spotting,
heading to soft ice-cream with twists
and sprinkles.

Later, hands sticky, tongues tidying
their cones, the girls serve up
silence for my free-range fable:
Summer days after lunch I'd bike to the pool—
who'd heard of seat belts or helmets?—
my tender brain laid bare as a
pumpkin to car tires, sun-splashed
hours swimming and diving, no SPF
to shield us, this Scots-Irish skin crisped
nearly to the bone, burst burns on
my shoulders rubbed raw as I slept.
Nights before the fireflies lit, we kids
chased the DDT truck, danced in
the smoky, gray billows blown from the
back, mouths open to swallow its secret—

how the poison cloud could keep us
safe from mosquitos and malaria.

Rinsing sugar from their mouths
with their BPA-free water bottles,
the girls signal they'll say my
unsaid: *Sounds awful—dangerous,*
primitive, like the Stone Age.

We wheel our way home, pedalling
past my Paleolithic Era and into
their future—the Plastiocene Age,
their beloved polar bears
drifting toward extinction,
floods rushing past the fires.

I

Series for My Mother

1 East Falls—Philadelphia, 1937

Beatrice Lindy Hops
with her boyfriend in my parents'
bright white kitchen, a place she scrubs
until even the radio shines. Its face looks
happy, sings Count Basie's orchestra.

Our maid is not my parents' pale
with blotchy reds, lines and freckles,
but the brown of Grace Kelly's help,
and smooth all over,
except for her hands.

She smells of licorice
drops and lemon oil and snuff, too,
father says, pooching out the skin
under her lower lip.

Beatrice's white apron is starched,
scratching me when she holds me,
cleaning my face and neck with
chamois cloth. She scrubs me
in her own bathroom tub,
then rubs me with
Jergens, cherry and almond.

On her bed which mother calls
a twin I stretch out beside her
in the small, brown room
mother named "Cup of Cocoa."

Beatrice and I know how hot and sticky
we will become tonight, the ceiling fan
whirring, and I will watch it as I throw
Miss Bea's clean white sheet up
over our heads and feel its cool breeze
before the soft cotton
settles slowly
and quietly on our skin.

2 Cuttings—Tyrone, 1952

When my new husband confessed
to cutting down
ten tender pink dogwoods that fall
as he cleared my parents' land
to build our house,
I could not know
how I would miss that loveliness come spring.

By April we were settled.
I curled into the cold commode
spitting up saltines and watching
blue veins brighten my white breasts,
as if pulsing to the surface.

Though I roughened the nipples with a washcloth,
I could not stand the newborn's mouth
sucking my swollen skin,
so slipped
a bottle between his gums.

David wailed while I rocked him and sang,
pulling his spindly, bowed legs
to his tummy in pain as I wept
and wondered why babies were drawn
asleep and smiling on pastel mounds of clouds.

When Betty Wilder returned
from college over Christmas,
heavy and depressed,

we pushed my baby buggy all over Hillcrest,
bundled against the knife-like wind,
across acres of farmland stench.

The baby sleeping brought
Betty's turn to cry
and stare, her scarred over wrists
calling out to my loneliness,
her tales of silent dates with vain boys
and hours with textbooks a wound to me.

Now I am thinking of when the budding will begin.
In bed, I picture myself
in those black capris and huaraches,
cherry red mouth pouting
for the camera,
sunning my face on the front stoop,
our coal-black spaniel dropping
a freshly killed baby bunny
at my feet.

3 Keeping Christmas—Tyrone, 2015

In the dark afternoons
I want to wrap up in my robe
and sleep forever.

"We must keep Christmas,"
Bill always said, and so I haul the tree
from the attic and fix the top to the bottom,
force the fake branches
to creak into place.

The tiny white lights bob like my palsied hand.
With my good hand, I stand
the damn thing in the bay window,
lean into my walker, plant
my feet to balance as I do
at Silver Sneakers.

"We'll have real spruce trees
until they carry me out of here feet first,
Bill also said." But we got this one
when his mind went, pacing the house,
conducting *The Messiah* and Dave Brubeck
to the music in his head.

The house down the hill, gaudy
with plastic mangers and carnival lit crosses,
cues my vertigo,
so I must sit to steady myself.

Tonight's meds line the end table
—aqua discs, bright pink circles
 and amber, gel ovals.
They keep me alive,
but don't cure my sorrow.

Swallowing so many,
I smile
as the gray pink and white
snowflakes on my robe blur
and I am a girl at William Penn

Charter skating pond,
crouching low
for my pancake spin,
feeling the ice solid
beneath my blades,
hair brushing my face,
hands tucked in my bunny fur muff,
and the December pines
whirling as I spin
then spot one,
its branches bending
with snow
and about to break.

A Daughter's Fish Story

The Washington School Fair
arrived each spring with the pollen.
I had never gone. Our family's summer
treat was a Jersey Shore week,
sharing a box of caramel corn the
final night on the boardwalk.

This year's fundraiser summoned
hopes for a buttery bag of my own,
of strolling the playground alone,
a sugary spool of cotton candy
a blue cloud in my hand.

The line for *Go Fishin'* hooked two
deep around the macadam playground.
I imagined bounty dangling on the end
of my pole: big-boobed, high-heeled
Barbies in boxes, Slinkies glimmering
gold in the late afternoon sun, makeup kits,
their pink pots shimmering, promising
growing up I could not yet envision.

I drop my ticket in the bowl and cast high
to clear the drawn drape, laughing to be
fishing dry land. Behind the barrier I feel
my line tug, hear my father whisper—
"Okay, reel in your fish."

Confused by how I can lift so high a
heavy toy as much as by the familiar
voice behind the curtain, I feel my face fold,

stunned, then crying with shame at the
pack of Juicy Fruit I have won for my
patience, for my faith in transformation.

When my mom asks if the school fair was
"everything I expected," I lie "Even better!,"
drawing my curtain between their world
and mine.

Dick And Jane at Play

Dark S-coils flowing,
orange stripes blazing,
its musk fails to scare us,
though stink sprays
my white Keds.

Snake! we scream,
more excited than
afraid, racing for a stick
to lift the
garter into a box
we litter with grass.

Our cousin Johnny,
woodskid kin,
kept his treasures in glass cubes,
slinging insects, toads and salamanders
for their suppers, building his reptiles a gym,
intricate levels of horizontals
and verticals
on which to sleep, climb, curl.

We have just a cardboard crate,
but prop a plank for ours
to furl but not escape.
Craving connection without
touch, we probe our prize
with the stake, admire its
long, white belly,
sleek, capped head,
black oval eyes.

How dutifully it climbs
our splintered stick,
then falls, its winding now
writhing, bin and grassy floor
smeared with gore.

We hide its house in the garage,
fold our guilt and worry
into tomorrow. I wipe the blood
from my hands to my
shorts, flee to my swing
in search of sky.

Saturday Night

My father steers our yellow Ford
Fairlane through the dark winter streets
of the hometown I did not yet

know was poor and broken—
what I would later describe,
as if to save myself from it,

as *rust-belt post-industrial.*
Past Gardner's Candy, we turn
toward the Juniata River,

rushing with melted snow
and sewage beside Hub
Pizza Place. Our town had two.

We had not yet heard the word
"Pizzeria." The server slides
our steaming box toward my father's

folded bills, the lit take-out window
revealing the muscled arms of
a man I knew to be Italian,

but did not yet know the connection
between him and my German
grandfather's *wop* sneer. I want now

to know why, driving home, my father
says the word *genes,* writes it in the cold
dust on the dashboard to explain

heredity, its boons and traps.
I sigh that my small parents had
made me small. Monday on the school

playground, I tell the girl whose father
owns West End Pizza that my dad
knows many things, such as *The Hub's*

best pizza crust. Big Brenda dwarfs
our whole school. Seconds later, this
giant hoists me above her head,

twirls me, dizzy and scared, and I
watch church spires and wooden
row homes, dirtied by mill dust,

repeat their pattern, what I
know now is a spiral of
downward recurrence.

Welsh Mythology

Each time my grandmother
bore at home
her thirteen children,
her legs spread wide,
bruised and bloodied
on the narrow bed,
back burning with labor
over twenty-two years,

my Welsh grandfather played his fiddle
as a birth announcement
in the cool dark of the parlor,
the coal town dim
behind lace curtains.

So many Smith tales told:
an arc of sweet myths
at Reservoir Park picnics.

Like my father's five year sucking
at Nannie's nipple,
wiping away the mustard
as she rocked and swayed him
to "The Highwayman,"
riding that *ribbon
of moonlight over the purple moor.*

Or how five Smith boys, a team,
shot baskets in the kitchen,
until Nannie, tired of weaving
among them to punch down her dough,
would swat them, send them off

with a "piece," bread thick with peach jam.
Smith lore banned darkness, it seems,
made sorrow a side note, like Aunt Ruth's
version of Aunt Jan who *died of leukemia,*
or we don't know what, at 21.

But Aunt Dot, wise and quiet
in her thin house dress
and soiled scuffs, framed this
slender story: Aunt Jan died
during an illegal abortion,
New York City, circa 1934.

Our plots join here
then divide. I thrived post abortion:
grad school, children,
teaching, only years later
waking in the night, mourning
a lost babe circling the earth,
longing to live.

Jan bled to death, her fetus,
like my own, a pink bud hacked
from our family tree. I replant
myth, give Rhiannon—Welsh queen,
horse goddess—water and air. Her
stolen son has always returned, as,
taken to the wind, she
blesses emptiness and births.

Ocean City, New Jersey

Crossing the Somers Point bridge,
the bay winks white and silver like
fish scales as my dead father rises

before me, snapping his fingers to
Earth, Wind and Fire, smiling and
nodding at convertibles and bikinis.

A blue-collar man working nights
in dim yellow light, but a guy
on vacation in madras and shades,

August 1973, bearing snowflake rolls
and sticky buns in greasy, yeasty bags
to his family's clapboard rental.

Today, Dad travels with my mother
and me in my *New Yorker* tote,
glad, we're hoping, to be back at

the Port-O-Call Hotel, its glamour
schmaltzy sweet, its towering pink
mass like a happy, cartoon whale.

The finger-painted horizon hovers
in blood-orange, while we walk our
husband and father to ocean's edge,

fling his heavy, gray-white ash to air
and water, watch bone blend with salt,
wash back to beginnings his clean pool break,

his brown sugar barbecue, his search for
the perfect peach, his smoke whispered into
our aching ears, his open laugh, his closed
sorrow.

Family Court

After the session in our courtroom,
some reported
that candles lit the dark, oil-stained garage.
I scrounged them from my grandmother's
dining room highboy,
behind the matches and Heath Bars,
for atmosphere, I assured my brother,
The Judge, just as I rounded up kids in
our neighborhood
promising Kool-Aid and pretzels after
The Verdict in Garage Court.

I had scammed judicial ritual
from *Perry Mason,* a show my bedtime
cut in half, just when the witness stand got heated.
At 11, my brother knew some law,
the term *judge's chambers,*
and that his church choir robe would,
in a pinch, stand in for his *judge's gown.*
That phrase whispered to me of *prom* mystery,
abstractions overheard from older cousins in
hushed conversations about *going steady,*
necking and parking.

My brother's solemn garb
corrected all that
as he strolled, somber,
into the courtroom,
holding his Bible against the folds
of his long, black robe,
head bent mock humble and low.
Already a practiced orator,

listening endlessly to
Everett Dirksen and JFK speeches
on a reel-to-reel,
my brother forced his tenor to barely baritone,
calling my cousin and me as witnesses,
nodding for the Myers' bunch,
picking their noses and mosquito bites
and asking about snacks,
to serve as silent jurors.

We were sorely prepared for motive,
crime, and defense, muffing lines, changing
our stories from murder to armed robbery.
The judge reddened and called a mistrial.

. . . .

In 2020, in a *blistering decision,*
said the NYT, a federal appeals court,
its Chief Judge my brother, rebuked
the petition of a litigious presidential
loser to reverse election results in
Pennsylvania thusly: *calling an*
election unfair does not make it so.
And each day I wrestle words,
each night light candles as witness.

II

My Mother's Pedicures

Though I nudge her toward plums
and apricots, she always chooses
proper pinks, reliable reds. I scoop
her into the mechanical chair,
the "C" of her stooped shoulders
and back massaged, azure water
and salts a hot whirlpool
salving her feet and legs.

You have the magic touch,
my mother tells every employee
of the pricey Discount Spa
who gingerly stroke and rub
her lower limbs, their faces furrowed,
worried, maybe, their thumbs might
push through her paper thin skin.

I have Parkinson's, you see,
so these pedicures work wonders
for my leg pain. It wakes me
up nights, my mother shouts
in English to Asian-American
women and men whose bilingual
skills and polite smiles and nods betray
neither her nor their gaps in understanding.

Sometimes she winces as they dig deep
into the beds of her toes, tweezing
shards of ingrown nail from her tender pads.
When her toenails have been brushed
with fuchsia, her callouses buffed *smooth,*
she chirps, *as a baby's bottom,* I lift her
into my car, holding the pain painted
beneath my mother's scarce pleasures.

Garvey Manor

A tiny dervish,
my mother whirled
around Assisted Living,
smiling and chatting
like a girl
running for homecoming queen.

Now pushing 90
she's no longer up at 5, sprinting
with her walker to fold her clean laundry
then read the local obituaries,
To make sure I am still alive!
Her body's pleasures and pains strike
their own balance these days.

She drags herself,
diapered and dripping,
out of bed at 10
and into her accessible shower,
sinking into her chair,
hot, soapy water stroking
her thighs and belly,
forgetting, finally,
her life-long utility budget.

Emerging naked through the steam,
blinking and sightless as a newborn,
she readies herself
for breakfast,
where she will spill
coffee down her pastel polo during a cat nap,

palsied hands trembling. She marvels
to me about her colleagues in suffering
and bingo. First Father Delgado,
legless, sacred air filling the space
where flesh should be,

but there he is, in his wheelchair,
grinning, buying cards in the gift shop,
or stretching his torso Heavenward
on the chinning bar at PT. *He's amazing.*
And there's Dottie—so teensy she slips

from chairs, but guess what? She wears
a size 10 shoe and birthed 10-pound boys,
up there on the mountain where she was a nurse.
And then so many get disappeared, it seems,
slumped and snacking during movie time one day

then I'm watching them carried out of here
the next, good and dead. You get used to it.
When we quarantined in March, nursing
staff cuts left hers a ghost town.

I can't remember the last time I had dry pants,
my mother laughs, still up for stoic schtick.
But they call me Sunshine here, you know,
others always complaining, but not me—not I.

Still, she thrills at the finches
darting, bickering,
picking at berries and,
she concedes, probably,
you know, mating.

The night before she dies
she's rhapsodic on the phone
about a beach day years back,
poking along the shore line,
our steps scattering plovers.

When I wake, my mother appears,
head bent low over her walker,
large breasts like pendulums pulling her
earthward, her body's gas and dust
rising as blinding sunlight.

Dancing With My Dead

My dead don't come to me in the
stillness of church, forest, corpse asana.

On occasion, they appear on beach walks,
tucking their mingled atoms tight in the

tides, leaving as waves crest or
recede. Sometimes on a bike or car

ride they slip in next to me, chat about
what they hear on NPR, ask about

dinner. It's motion that conjures
them, I'm sure, plus music, so

time with my dead loves blends
ballroom, Broadway, street dance party.

Mother favored head bobbing, singing
"Onward Christian Soldiers" with the

coiffed and blazered women of Episcopal
Trinity. As counterpoint, I grab her

to join me on WRTI's Latinx night,
moving together in samba, smiling at what

hips can do. She reddens then fades from
me here, so I move quickly into my best

Julie Andrews' "I Could Have Danced All Night,"
ladies, not women, mother's life theme.

Dad moves in, bringing her back, crooning
Sinatra sexy to "Moon River," grabbing

my hand for a turn before slipping
into "I'll Be Home for Christmas." I step

aside as my parents foxtrot, whisper about
oranges for Christmas, WWII, their own dead.

Cousin Don takes shape with his husband, Bud,
a non-dancer, so I know Donnie, eyes starry

with show tune glitz, will stiffly straight dance
with me to "There's A Place for Us," honoring

Bernstein, gay love and the night we
streamed *West Side Story,* clinging to one

another, sobbing with Natalie Wood's
Maria for our doomed darling, Tony.

Connie steps from the shade, bending low,
snapping her fingers a capella as she cool

steps toward me, our fifth grade Sharks
and Jets bit, then fingers meet fist for

her rock star mic, shaking her hair
as she belts "Baby we were bo-orn to run!"

Our eyes lock, arms beckoning, reeling the
other in with that 70's dance cliche. I want

return and hereafter: my 60's Dad singing
Simon & Garfunkel, surprising Don about

queer *Oklahoma!,* clubbing with Connie.
But my dead know better, jitterbugging

now in a circle, all of us trading partners
and grinning, singing "Ring Around the Rosie,"

then I am touching only my own skin.

House Aria

after Sharon Olds

Oh! How I have loved houses more than husbands,
coveted and owned them with working-class
pride wedding *West Elm* design.
The arts and crafts Dutch Colonial,
a Civil War Philly row home,
those strong bones holding a walled terrace
where once stood a carriage house.
Or the neo-Gothic Fairmount rehab
where, stepping from the shower
to a roof deck and outdoor kitchen
come evening, lifts me with the swifts,
swooping into the clouds.
Men's marriage vows meld together,
soon gone, one husband losing libido fast,
another slipping fidelity's collar with internet sex,
their workouts and pledges giving way to
paunches, to snoring, to their gray Februaries
of habit, their lust for the lissome,
the secret, the other. But how houses hold
their promise for decades! The dust and dirt
of demo filling our mouths, the worst price paid
for an 1800 basement reborn as "finished,"
pastel walls and dehumidified floor tile
dotted with weights, a sectional,
and a big screen. Witness that, indeed,
my house loves have stood steady, welcomed
my yearnings, yielded earth soft with rain
so that pulling pachysandra, invasive deadnettle,
and creeping myrtle seems kind, transformative
yet perennial, the muddy ground given
over to flagstone, beds thick with soft lavender,

domed night lights and the blowsy bending
of pink Cosmos. I have searched for this beauty,
these cycles of renewal in marriage.
I have longed to replace the tired with the true,
imagine still the grays, whites and blues
of our attic sky suite a Sistine Ceiling, calling my
husband and me, after the fall, to our restoration.

Ode to a Singular Phalaenopsis

Gifts grabbed from Giant or Lowe's—
moth orchids in dark peach, white,
shell pink, their delicate blooms wings,
fleshy labellum and lips
lascivious almost, an O'Keefe

parody of whorled lady parts.
Their flowers fell
without regrowth. Each time
I grieved, waited weeks,
months
for buds,
for my princess
to awake, to make

Mapplethorpe statements,
spread sparse beauty
across mantel and desk,
nod subtly to taste,
to vitality.

I study friends' success,
read recipes for orchid health:
under water, water weekly,
more sun,
diffused light, benign
neglect, eggshell compost,
fertilizer from the Philippines.

I wait for rebloom, nurture these
nodes in an empty womb, cut
stalk back, hold hands
to heart's center, wonder if wine
would work. Then the trash.

44

Back from insanity's ledge,
my husband arrives at fall
equinox with another Phalaenopsis.
I eye them both with dread
and doubt, water them without
a smidge of hope or trust,
only another living thing
willing others weal and life.

For him there's lithium, lamotrigine
and soup. The orchid gets my sitting
room sill, long light, a dearth of love.
Flowers hold until Halloween,
then drop each day for a week.

By Thanksgiving, glossy green buds
line the stalk like pupae, grow fat,
tease me with
soft slips of pale flesh
pushing from the inside. Eight lilac
veined, pale blossoms burst, one
by one. The stalk splits,
offers a new stem of flower heads.

His mania dormant,
my mate and I bear
silent witness to this turn.
Our orchid grows heavy,
an arc of snowy clusters,
its long, crescent neck bending low,
a swan flush with grace.

Waking in Cluis

I tumble out
of that nightmare rerun:
my babies gone,

morphed again into
bugs or dust at my breast.
I find you sipping sugared

coffee, your face sweet
with sleep in the still,
dark dining room.

We wander this storybook
town's winding, cobbled
streets, their shuttered houses

and geranium boxes neat as
nursery rhymes. You are drawn
to the art of the charcuteries,

whose windows gleam with
tubes of glistening red sausage,
hares hung by their twined back

legs, eyes still shining, front legs
stretching as if to leap back to life.
Across the street, boulangeries

with their yeasty promise, their
alchemy of flour, butter and sugar
float like longing in the morning air.

Beside them *la petite epicerie,*
its stalls filled with tiny field
strawberries, nectarines like nipples,

green apples, nestled and small.
These will feed those Shetlands,
grazing with their parents, nuzzling

and chasing each other under last
night's milky moon. We bite pieces
of tart, crisp fruit, toss them under

the fence, yearn, instead, for communion,
for lush equine licks cleansing
our cupped hands.

Flies circle the ponies, whose gaze turns us
to the gray stone of the lane's
crucifix, whose wounds,

outstretched arms and lowered head
appear like a welcome,
a way to waken.

The Social Contract

The envelopes drop daily to the foyer floor, the door's mail mouth
clapping shut, demanding the usual ransom: give today to Save the
Children the suicidal Africa's Wildlife everyone's bees literacy
Monarchs women's reproductive rights public radio Philabundance
trans-youth the Human Rights Campaign Audubon's Near Extinct
the multiplying homeless you can make a difference to Doctors
Without Borders or to correct cleft lips genital mutilation
Republican gerrymandering the oceans' plastic swamps police
brutality against communities of color not to mention men walking
or driving while black or donate now to Indigenous Education
Susan G. Komen breast cancer Habitat for Humanity The Salvation
Army Salvadoran and Honduran migrants all of this follows me
floor to floor today tomorrow next month past 2030 when fuel
emission standards will be reduced globally so my grandchildren's
children might inhabit a blue-green planet but only if I give
generously which I've clearly done too often to compound these
appeals but I can't just recycle Nancy Pelosi's alarmed pleas about
Trump's 2024 war chest all news of the starving poached kill
sheltered or shivering outside in winter pups people whose new
hearts lungs kidneys might fly to them—housed in a cooler on ice,
as if the harvested organs were traveling happily to a family picnic–
but only today with my help. My role exhausts me. Most often I
pull the pile from the big blue bin, bump it to the second floor
wicker basket, where social need and species' survival live for
weeks or months, gathering guilt like dust in my office.

Two Therapists and a Poet Walk into a Bar

I. Releasing Tension

Nafi's hands move
up her back
like a master potter,
smoothing coils of muscle,
arriving at the nape,
pushing and pulling flesh
to a thin rim as he lifts
the stem, lays a rolled and
steaming cloth beneath her neck.

He gestures now with his own body,
a model as tall and taut
as a Gray's Anatomy sketch,
schooling her in posture to
release tension. She practices
in agony at home.

II. Holding Tension

Amy celebrates a dialectical
dance, coaching her clients
to balance polarities
as equal truths:
to hold tension between
loving and loathing our mates,
dreading visits with our dying
or demented parents, even
as we ache to keep them here.

Shaking free of her college
crush on Hegel and synthesis,
she links the cerebrum and limbic
system together as a tightrope
to carry the yin and yang of being:
her sad son, his last, lost decades
a holding cell, hostage to inertia,
rages, depression, then prison,
though her pole's
poised,
reaching across the highwire,
holding his soccer and hockey
star chest bumps, his laughter
at *I Love Lucy* on *Nick at Night,*
his damp, blond head bent over a book.

III. Being and Time

Then holding her disciplined life
and own wildness
in equipoise with the scant
years left:
to switchback Bryce Canyon,
hoodoos stacked and glittering,
cut shortbread stars at Christmas
set in gift box constellations,
bike along the Schuylkill River,
Canada geese weaving their
southward skein. Bearing this
tension causes pain. Then it gets easier.

Wave

They're living in the basement
these 110 degree days,
pushing their Extra King mattress,
folded like a crepe, down the
rotting stairs, the dogs leading
and following, yipping then whining.
They all sleep down there,
together in "The Bunker."

Mildew makes itself known every
night in their coughing. Hunched
over the weed bowl before bed,
then lifting to exhale, she pictures
the mold as a goofy, horned, wild thing.
When he's not on his medication,
he sees it as Charles Manson.

Rising at 6:30 to prep for kiddie
horse camp, her bra and thong
slippery with sweat, she wonders if
anyone in Portland can sleep, these
temperatures not Pacific, not Northwest,
arriving as part of The Change.

Before she presses her coffee,
she stands on the old kitchen stool
to pull alive the ceiling fan,
its dust and dead insects flying
from the blades like dark fairies
lighting on the clean, white counter.

He will sleep most of the morning
as she sprays water like salvation
on the kids under the trees,
the Shetlands and Trotters dipping
their heads, frothy with saliva,
in pails of recycled rain, while he

smokes his first cigarette of the day.
He swallows his Seroquel, then leashes
the Husky and Rottweiler together,
all of them climbing the asphalt road
above the highway, watching the cars
shimmering in the heat as the light
bends, waiting for her return.

Birds of Philadelphia

More than half the world's sapiens
live in cities. Concrete a common
groundcover, we forgo private gardens,
birdfeeders, overhyped lawns
for human culture—theatre, art,
street—and nightlife.

On our best days, the Delaware River
calls us to look up, ghostly white gulls
gliding toward Jersey, or down,
along the Schuylkill, fluffy, Dijon-
flecked goslings tottering underfoot.
Street sparrows brawling over
pizza crust or taking dust baths serve
our daily biodiversity. No one moves
to a city to birdwatch.

That was the Aughts and Teens.
When dinner parties reconvened,
we entertained one another with tales
of what we'd survived, or not,
questions epochal and Biblical.
Were the Spotted Lanternflies a sign,
hitchhiking across the counties a few
years back, sucking on sap that morphed
to deadly tree mold? We mused on where
our post-plague signifiers might emerge.
Bird stories fluttered back and forth across the table:

Temple's 90.1 sang praise for thousands
of robins wrestling worms in the wet earth
across campus; a Merion teacher
saw scores of Cooper hawks
gripping tree branches along 76 East;

a South Philly plumber claimed a conclave
of cardinals nesting beneath roof decks,
flashes of red through the air like
flamenco-dancing fathers. Finches
by the dozens painted the stone walls
at Eastern State with yellow motion
singing among the thistles. The hostess
dishes up a final tale: *Back from Hot Yoga,*
I stopped short as two white doves huddled
on my window ledge, their cries a love language,
dirge, the seventh seal?

Winged creatures our secular angels,
trillions of Brood X cicadas surfaced
in days, tymbal organs thrumming from
Georgia to New York and westward,
eating, mating, aerating the soil,
their dead bodies dusted into nitrogen,
their prophecy: to reverse
our damned dominion.

The Big Dipper

That May night on our roof deck
when I exchanged our dirty
dinner plates
for a freezing bottle of French bubbles,
the sky turned navy purple.
Ursa Major, my husband murmured.
The curtain open,
I lift my face to watch the show,
champagne stars bursting inside
my lips, nose and throat,
the great ladle pouring light
and heat on our gazing.

About the Author

VA Smith lives in Fairmount, Philadelphia, her adopted city, where she reads and writes, walks and bikes, serves as a home chef/caterer, and loves on her family and friends.

VA has published in several dozen literary journals and anthologies, among them: *Blue Lake Review, Ginosko Literary Journal, MacQueen's Quinterly, Mobius, Quartet, The Southern Review, Verdad, Third Wednesday, and* forthcoming in *Evening Street Review and West Trade Review.* She is currently finishing a collection titled *America's Daughters & Other Poems,* enabling her to ignore her Peleton way more than advisable.

www.ingramcontent.com/pod-product-compliance
Lightning Source LLC
Chambersburg PA
CBHW031153090426
42738CB00008B/1316